Boost Creative Writing

Planning Sheets to Support Writers (Especially SEN Pupils) in Years 1–2

Judith Thornby

We hope you and your pupils enjoy using the ideas in this book. Brilliant Publications publishes many other books to help primary school teachers. To find out more details on all of our titles, including those listed below, please go to our website: www.brilliantpublications.co.uk.

Boost Creative Writing – Years 3–4	978-1-78317-059-3
Boost Creative Writing – Years 5–6	978-1-78317-060-9
Brilliant Activities for Reading Comprehension, Year 1	978-1-78317-070-8
Brilliant Activities for Reading Comprehension, Year 2	978-1-78317-071-5
Brilliant Activities for Reading Comprehension, Year 3	978-1-78317-072-2
Brilliant Activities for Reading Comprehension, Year 4	978-1-78317-073-9
Brilliant Activities for Reading Comprehension, Year 5	978-1-78317-074-6
Brilliant Activities for Reading Comprehension, Year 6	978-1-78317-075-3
Brilliant Activities for Creative Writing, Year 1	978-0-85747-463-6
Brilliant Activities for Creative Writing, Year 2	978-0-85747-464-3
Brilliant Activities for Creative Writing, Year 3	978-0-85747-465-0
Brilliant Activities for Creative Writing, Year 4	978-0-85747-466-7
Brilliant Activities for Creative Writing, Year 5	978-0-85747-467-4
Brilliant Activities for Creative Writing, Year 6	978-0-85747-468-1
Developing Reading Comprehension Skills Years 5-6: Classic Children's Literature	978-0-85747-837-5
Developing Reading Comprehension Skills Years 5-6: Classic Poetry	978-0-85747-846-7
How to Achieve Outstanding Writers in the EYFS and KS1	978-0-85747-838-2
Cracking Creative Writing	978-0-85747-831-3
Boost Spelling Skills	978-0-85747-803-0

Published by Brilliant Publications Limited
Unit 10
Sparrow Hall Farm
Edlesborough
Dunstable
Bedfordshire
LU6 2ES, UK

www.brilliantpublications.co.uk

The name Brilliant Publications and the logo are registered trademarks.

Written by Judith Thornby
Illustrated by Cathy Hughes
Cover illustration by Frank Endersby
Designed by Brilliant Publications Limited

© Text Judith Thornby 2014
© Design Brilliant Publications Limited 2014

Printed book ISBN: 978-1-78317-058-6
E-book ISBN: 978-1-78317-061-6

First printed and published in the UK in 2014

The right of Judith Thornby to be identified as the author of this work has been asserted by herself in accordance with the Copyright, Designs and Patents Act 1988.

Pages 6–73 may be copied by individual teachers acting on behalf of the purchasing institution for classroom use only, without permission from the publisher and without declaration to the Copyright Licensing Agency or Publishers' Licensing Services. The materials may not be reproduced in any other form or for any other purpose without the prior permission of the publisher.

Contents

Introduction	4
Links to the National Curriculum	5
Suggested writing targets	6

Adventure story

Fifi and the beanstalk	7
Fifi and the snake	8
Fifi and the dog	9
Fifi and the pull-along dog	10
Sam and the Queen	11
Sam and the dragon egg	12
Sam and the cross crab	13
Freddie Frog	14
The Queen pops out	15–16
The magic carpet	17
Toto's adventure	18
The red balloon	19–21
Stuck on the island	22–23

Descriptive account

About me	24
My home	25
My dad	26
My mummy	27
My friend	28
Who am I?	29
My day as a Victorian child	30
My dream party	31
Autumn – I can see	32–33

Fairy tale

Create a fairy tale	34–35
Create a character for a fairy tale	36–37
Create a setting for a fairy tale	38–39

Fantasy

The super mini-beast	40
My pet monster	41–42
It's time to go out	43–44

Information report

Our trip to the seaside	45
Victorian seaside	46
The story of Grace Darling	47–48
The story of Emily Davison	49–50
The story of Rosa Parks	51–52
Christopher Columbus	54–54
The first man on the moon	55–56

Letter/Review

A letter to Santa	57–58
Book review	59
A review of Year 2	60

Poetry

Rain	61–62
My home	63
Grandad	64–65
Fireworks	66–67
Mini-beasts	68–69
Spring	70–71

Templates

Story mountain template	72
Mind map template	73

Introduction

These series of planning sheets aim to provide a structured resource which gives plenty of scope for exploring and collecting ideas in the different writing genres: adventure, fantasy, recount, letter, poetry etc. They generate discussion within a defined framework and then aid pupils to write more descriptive stories and compose longer pieces of writing.

Reluctant writers or those writers who struggle with the organization of their ideas can express themselves with more self-assurance by using these planning sheets. Confident writers can also benefit by delving into them to gain further ideas.

Some sheets can be written on directly but many are designed as a prop to refer to when writing. Vocabulary sheets are incorporated with some stories to help the flow of ideas.

Story mountain and mind map templates are included to assist narrative and descriptive writing and to cater for different learning styles. Visual learners have lots of imaginative ideas but might struggle with the sequence of events or the bare skeleton of the story so can benefit from using the story mountain approach. Logical systematic learners can sequence ideas but might struggle to develop them creatively and can benefit from using the mind map templates to expand descriptive writing.

I have specialized in the field of learning support since 1997 when I gained a diploma in specific learning difficulties. I am especially interested in promoting creative writing skills with children who are reluctant writers or who struggle with the organization of their ideas. These series of planning sheets generate discussion and aid in structuring composition in the different writing genres. They also can be used to give further ideas to confident writers as well. I have found that they have been successful in giving pupils greater self-assurance to express themselves in written form and have helped to make writing an enjoyable experience!

On page 5 you will see how the activities in the book link to the 2014 National Curriculum for England. On page 6 there are suggested writing targets. The way I use these is to cut out the relevant one(s) and tape them to the top of the sheets prior to copying, so that pupils have the targets in front of them as they work.

Links to the National Curriculum

The sheets in **Boost Creative Writing** will help Year 1 and 2 pupils to develop their composition skills, as set out in the National Curriculum for England (2014).

Year 1 – Composition

It is important for children to talk about what they are going to write prior to attempting to put their ideas on paper. The sheets in **Boost Creative Writing** are designed to do just that.

Through talking about what they want to write about, children can be encouraged to compose sentences orally and sequence their ideas to form short narratives. The adventure story sheets, in particular, encourage pupils to think about the structure of the story – what happens next? And then? What happens at the end?

After pupils have finished writing, encourage them to talk about what they have written with you or other pupils and to check that what they have written makes sense.

Reading their writing aloud helps children to see that their writing is valued. The poetry sheets are particularly good for this.

Year 2 – Composition

The sheets in **Boost Creative Writing** provide opportunities for pupils to write a range of different types of writing, from narratives and descriptive accounts, to information reports on real events and poetry. They will not only learn how to write for different purposes, they will also develop stamina for writing. Some of the information reports link to the History Programme of Study.

The sheets are designed to encourage children to talk about what they are going to write prior to doing so. The sheets provide opportunities for children to jot down ideas and key words. Many of the sheets have ideas and vocabulary that will act as prompts to stimulate pupils to discuss, prior to writing, what they want to say and how best to say it.

The design of the sheets, with boxes for each sentence or key idea, will aid children in putting their thoughts in order and help them to structure their writing in a logical way.

Pupils should be encouraged to re-read their work and make simple additions, revisions and corrections. Reading their writing aloud, to a teacher or other pupils, is a particularly valuable way of helping pupils to notice where and how their writing could be improved. In addition to checking for errors in spelling, grammar and punctuation, they should also be encouraged to check consistency of verb tenses.

As with Year 1, pupils should be encouraged to read their work aloud, with appropriate intonation.

Vocabulary, grammar and punctuation

Many of the sheets contain suggested vocabulary to encourage children to extend their range of vocabulary and prompt them to use new words in their writing. All the activities can also be used to reinforce children's understanding of grammar and punctuation, but this is not the primary purpose of the sheets.

Suggested writing targets

	Relates to
To remember to start a sentence with a capital letter	Any
To put a full stop at the end of every sentence	Any
To use full sentences in my writing	Any
To use capital letters and full stops in my story	Any story
To leave finger spaces between words	Any
To use 3 WOW words in my story	Any story
To use the words 'one day', 'then' and 'finally' in my story	Any story
To start some of my sentences with these words: Then... After that... Suddenly... Next minute... Finally...	Any story
To link sentences using the word 'because' in my writing	Any
To link sentences using some of these words in my writing: 'because', 'but', 'and', 'so', 'until'	Any
To use different words for 'ran' in 'Toto's adventure' story: hopped, jumped, scuttled, scampered, scurried	Toto's adventure
To use adjectives in my writing	Any
To start my story with an interesting sentence	Any story
To write a story with a beginning, middle and an ending	Any story
To plan my character description by drawing a picture and adding adjectives before writing	Fairy tale My pet monster
To write a magical fairytale, thinking about setting and character	Fairy tale
To describe myself as well as possible using WOW words	About me Who am I?
To use 5 WOW words in a detailed description of a pet monster	My pet monster
To play around with NOISY words and make up a firework poem	Fireworks
To start each line of my poem with a capital letter	Any poem
To use rhyming words in my 'Rain' poem	Rain
To use these words in a poem about a mini-beast: Next to... Under... Beside... In... On... Near...	Mini-beasts
To write 4–5 super sentences in my description of autumn	Autumn – I can see
To write a book review, including a short description of the main character and plot as well as my view of the book	Book review

This page may be photocopied for use by the purchasing institution only.

Fifi and the beanstalk

One day
What does Fifi do?

Then
What does Fifi do?

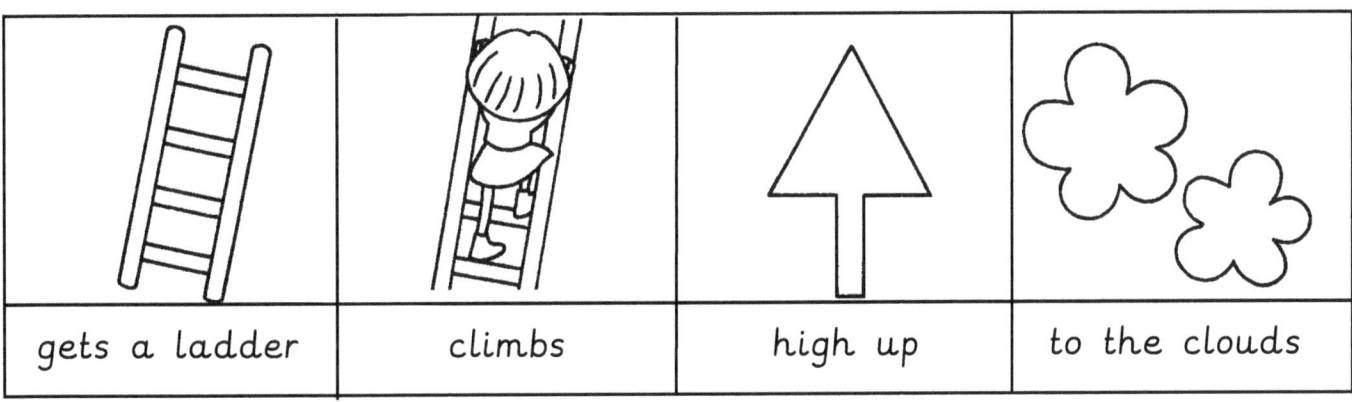

After that
What does Fifi find? What is it full of?

Finally
What happens at the end?

Fifi and the snake

One day
What does Fifi do?

| wakes up | sunny day | puts on her skates |

Then
What happens?

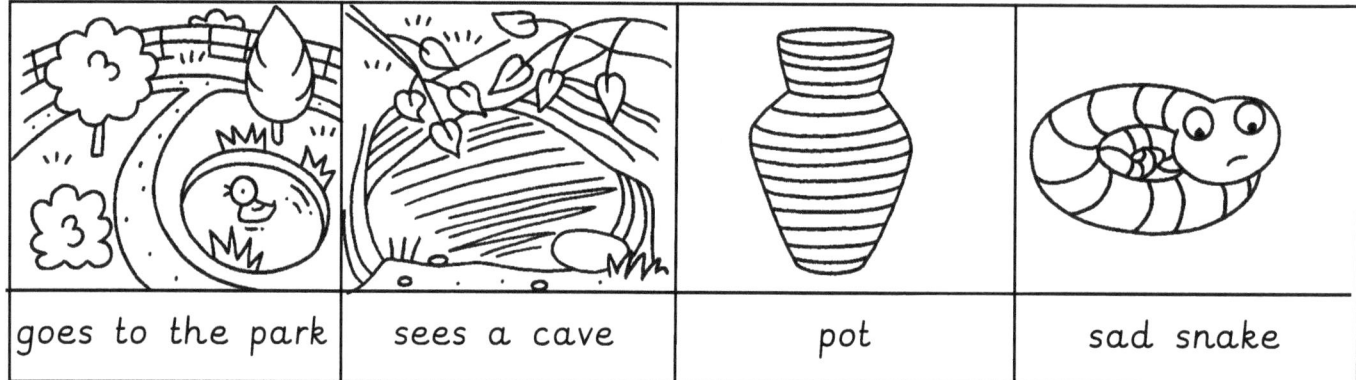

| goes to the park | sees a cave | pot | sad snake |

After that
What does Fifi do?

gives it	a cake	to eat

Finally
What happens at the end?

Fifi and the dog

One day
What does Fifi do?

| goes to the park | plays with her teddy bear | kicks the ball | water |

Then
What happens?

| dog | runs into water | gets wet | Fifi says |

After that
What happens next?

Finally
What happens at the end?

| Useful words | | | | | | | | | |
| the | with | it | and | they | she | into | go | home | |

Fifi and the pull-along dog

One day
What does Fifi do?

wakes up | gets her toy dog | pulls it outside

Then
What happens?

sees a door | pushes it open | stops at a tree

After that
What does Fifi do?

a wizard is by the tree | waves a magic wand

Finally
Fifi's pull-along dog becomes real!

Sam and the Queen

One day
What does Sam do?

Then
What does Sam do?

After that
What happens next?

Finally
What happens at the end?

Sam and the dragon egg

One day
What does Sam do?

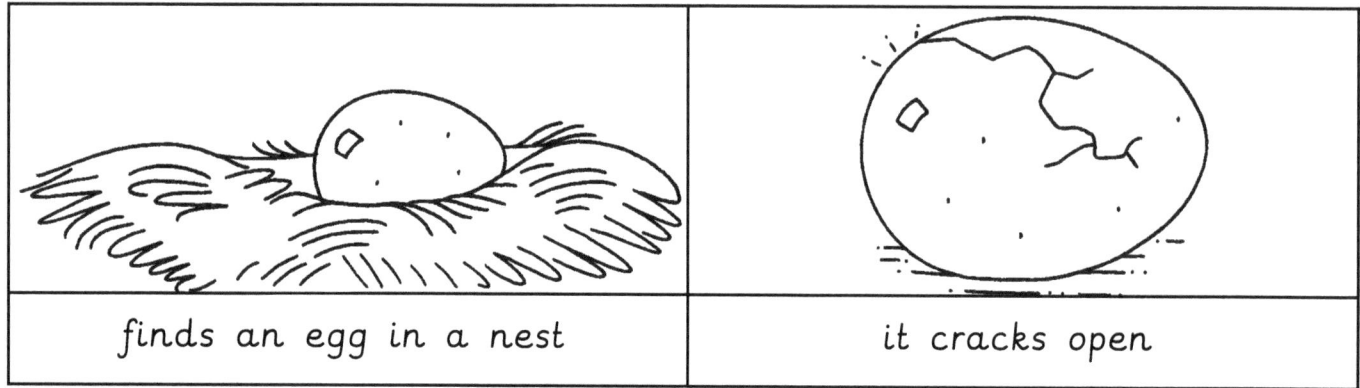

| finds an egg in a nest | it cracks open |

Then
What happens?

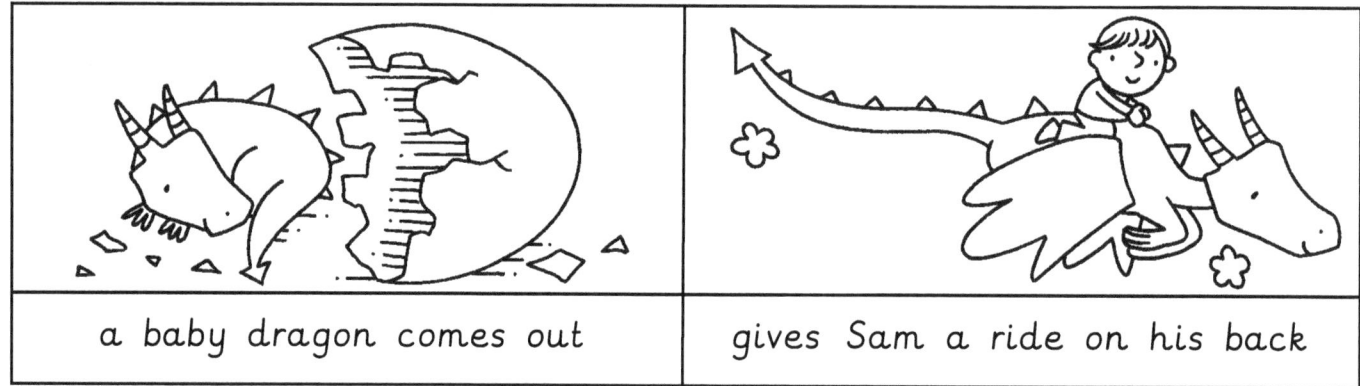

| a baby dragon comes out | gives Sam a ride on his back |

After that
What happens next?

| Where do they go? | What do they see? |

Finally
What happens at the end?

Sam and the cross crab

One day
What does Sam do?

| gets his spade | digs in the sand | finds a crab |

Then
What does he do?

puts it in a bucket

After that
Then what happens?

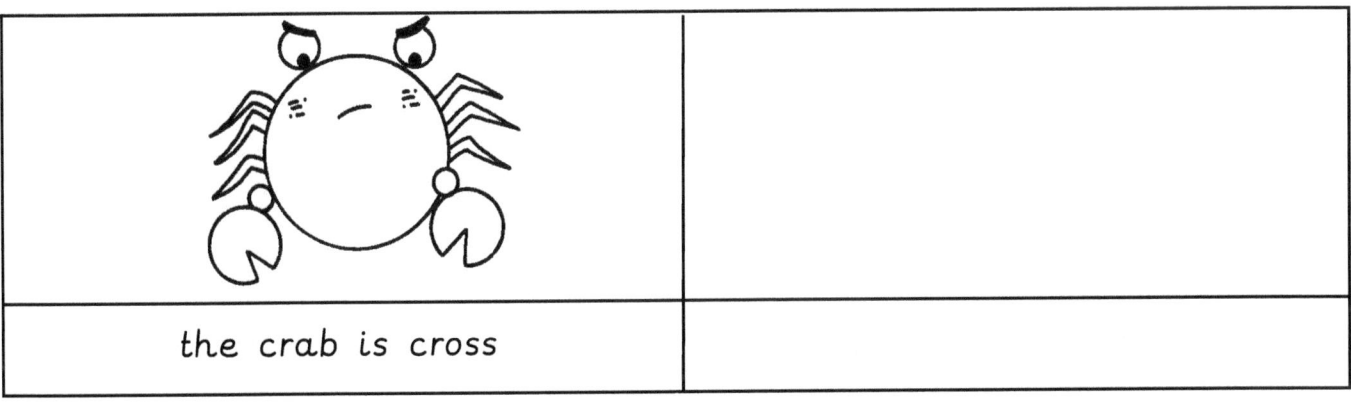

the crab is cross

Finally
What happens at the end?

Freddie Frog

One day
What does Freddie Frog do?

Then
What happens?

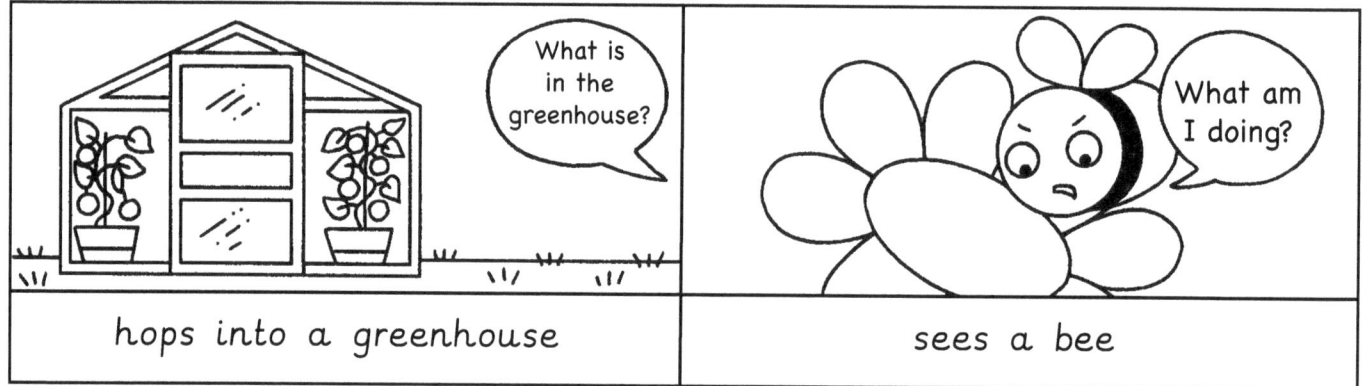

After that
What does Freddie do?

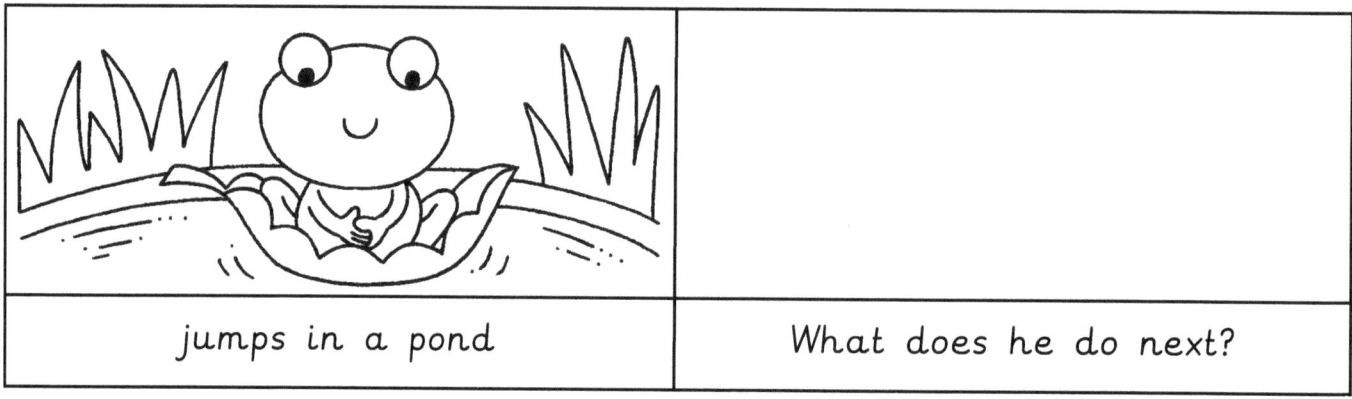

Finally
What happens in the end?

The Queen pops out

One day
The Queen pops out of the palace in disguise.

| she puts on an old... | she dyes her hair... | she will not wear her... | she will not take her... |

Then
What happens?

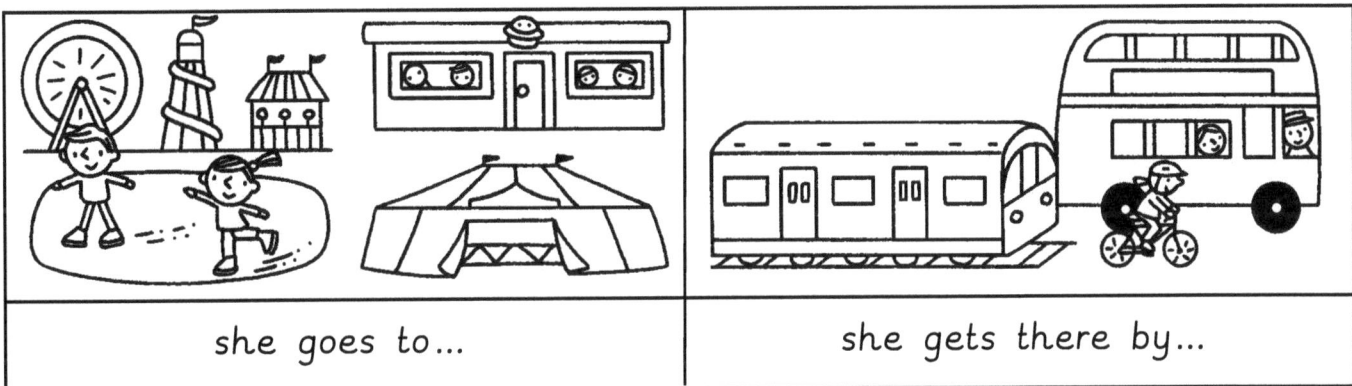

| she goes to... | she gets there by... |

After that
What happens?

| while she is there she... | and then she... |

Finally
She goes back to the palace. She has had a _____ time.

Will she go out in disguise again?

Boost Creative Writing, Years 1–2
© Judith Thornby and Brilliant Publications Limited

The Queen pops out

Use some of these words to help you write your story.

hair
red
black
brown
dress coat
wig
pair of
  sunglasses

crown jewels
carriage
corgis

bus
walks
rides on a bicycle
train
underground

shopping centre
ice rink
zoo
circus
McDonalds
fun fair

buys a hat
skates round the rink
sees an elephant
eats a burger
has a ride on the dodgems

fantastic
great day
good fun

The magic carpet

Write a story about someone who found a magic carpet and could go for a ride on it anywhere in the world.

Who?
Where did the person find the carpet?
What did it look like?

Ideas: in the attic   in a shop   at the back of an old wardrobe

---

What happened next? Then?
What could the person see?

Ideas: floated up in the air   zoomed   whizzed

Where did the magic carpet take the person?

Ideas: amusement park   seaside   the moon

Write about two or more things that happened there.
What did the person bring home?

Finally
What happened to the carpet?
Was it ever used again?
What did the person think about the trip?

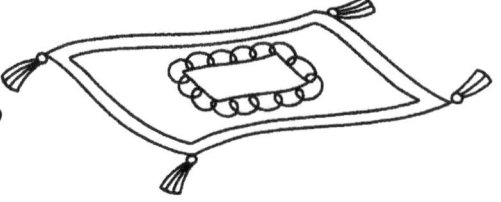

Toto's adventure

When Toto, the big white school rabbit, woke up, he noticed that his hutch door had not been shut properly. He ran off to see what was going on.

He hopped into the school garden.
What did he see? What did he hear?

After that?
He scampered into...

Ideas: the store cupboard   reception class   school office

Who did he meet?
What did he see? How did he feel?

What did he smell coming from the kitchen?
Did he eat something?

Finally
Toto went back to his hutch because...

Would Toto like to have another adventure?

The red balloon

Adventure story

Bobby, the big red balloon, floated high up into the sky. He floated into _____'s garden.
(your name)

What could Bobby see and hear in your garden?
He could see...   He could also see...
He could hear...

Ideas: trampoline   swing   cat   dog   bee   friend   brother

Then he floated to _____
(where you live)

What could he see and hear in your town/village?
He could see...
He could hear...

Ideas: bus   train station   baker's shop   postbox   fair

Then he floated to _____
(your school)

What could he see and hear?
He could see...
He could hear...

Ideas: playground   teacher   slide   pond   caretaker

Finally
What happened to Bobby the balloon?

Ideas: popped   landed safely (where?)

Boost Creative Writing, Years 1–2
© Judith Thornby and Brilliant Publications Limited

This page may be photocopied for use by the purchasing institution only.

The red balloon

Draw, colour and label a mind map of ideas.

What could it see?   hear?   smell?

In my garden

In my town/village

At school

The red balloon

Read this story to generate some ideas.

One day Bobby the red balloon floats high up into the air. There is a fluffy cloud in the blue sky. He hears an aeroplane pass by. He looks down into Yassin's garden. He hears a busy bee buzzing in the garden. It is getting some nectar from a flower so it can make some honey. He can see a washing line and there are two red socks and a blue shirt on the line. He sees Yassin, who is nine years old, kicking a football. Yassin's dog, Rocky is chasing a little black cat into the house. Then he floats across to Anytown. He hears a train roaring into the station. He can see a cake shop and he smells some delicious chocolate cookies that have just come out of the oven. He drifts across to Any School. He can hear lots of children laughing in the playground. A girl called Molly is sliding down a slide. Then a teacher called Mrs McCooke blows the whistle and Molly has to line up with her class. Finally Bobby balloon floats down to the ground. He lands on a prickly leaf and suddenly he goes POP!

Further suggestions

◆ Use props – a balloon (helium if possible) and pictures as prompts to oral retelling of the story. Possible pictures: cloud, aeroplane, bee, washing line, dog, football, train, chocolate cookies, slide, whistle, holly).
◆ Make sure that pupils are using full sentences when orally recounting each part of the story.
◆ Emphasize using words 'Then…', After that…', 'Suddenly…', 'Finally…'
◆ Pupils to draw pictures for their own stories (help them to label with descriptive words as required) and ensure pupils use these pictorial sheets as an aid when writing.

Stuck on the island

Write a story about two children who have rowed their boat to an island and got stuck on it when the boat disappeared.

It was a beautiful sunny day and the sea was very calm – just the sort of day to visit the island.

Who are the children?
How do they get across to the island?

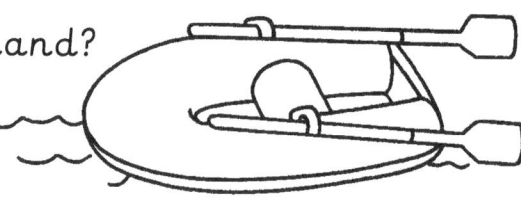

Write about three things they did when they got to the island.

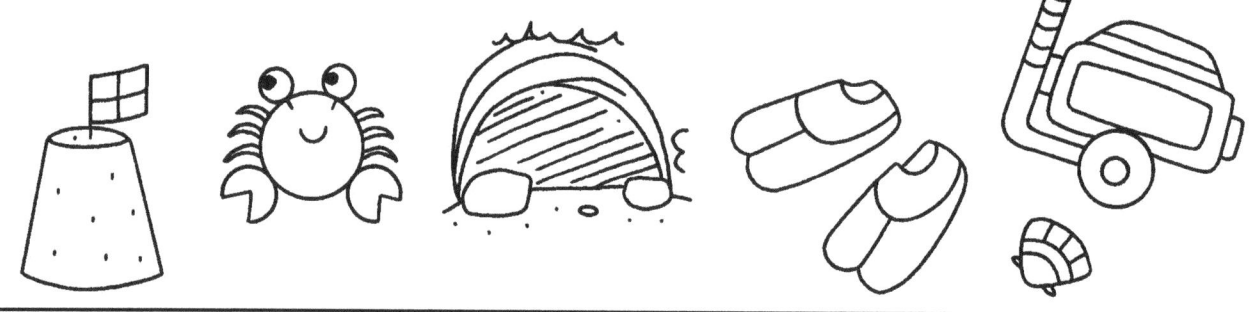

What did they have for their picnic lunch?

    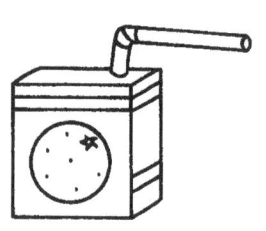

What did they do when they discovered their boat had gone?
How did they feel?
What happened next?
Who came to their rescue?

Finally
When they were back home, their mum said…

Stuck on the island

Use some of these words to help you write your story.

packed a picnic
rowed the boat to the island

built a sandcastle	went for a swim
rock pools	explored
caught a big crab	found a cave

sat down for lunch	
sandwiches	apple
ham	banana
cheese	biscuit
crisps	cake
juice	orange squash

wanted to go home	heard noise
noticed	sound of
boat disappeared	lifeboat
looked everywhere	helicopter
upset	dolphin
felt worried	happy
	relieved
	rescued

After a while...
Next minute...
Suddenly...
Eventually...
Then...
At last...

 Descriptive account

About me

I am _____ years old.

I have _____ sister(s) and _____ brother(s).

0 1 2 3 4 5 6 7 8 9

This is my drawing of me.

I have

Ideas: rabbit(s)   fish   cat(s)   dog(s)

I like to

My home

I live in a _____ .

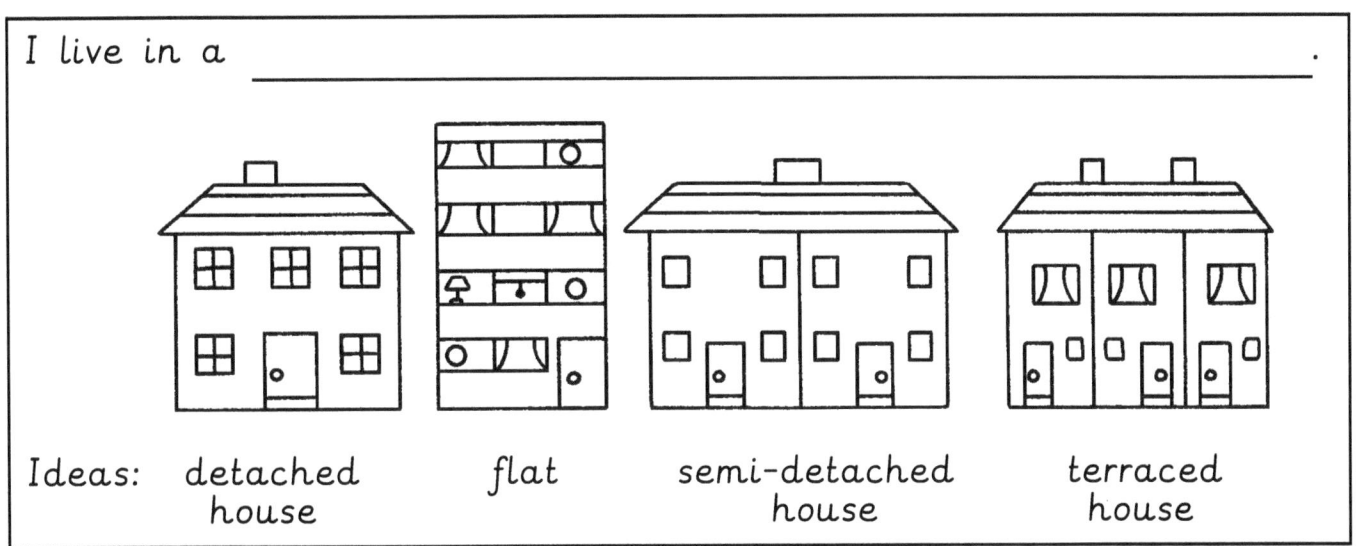

Ideas: detached house, flat, semi-detached house, terraced house

It has _____ bedrooms.

Ideas: one, two, three, four, five

My home has got a

Ideas:
garage, garden
chimney, extension
study, kitchen

This is my drawing of where I live.

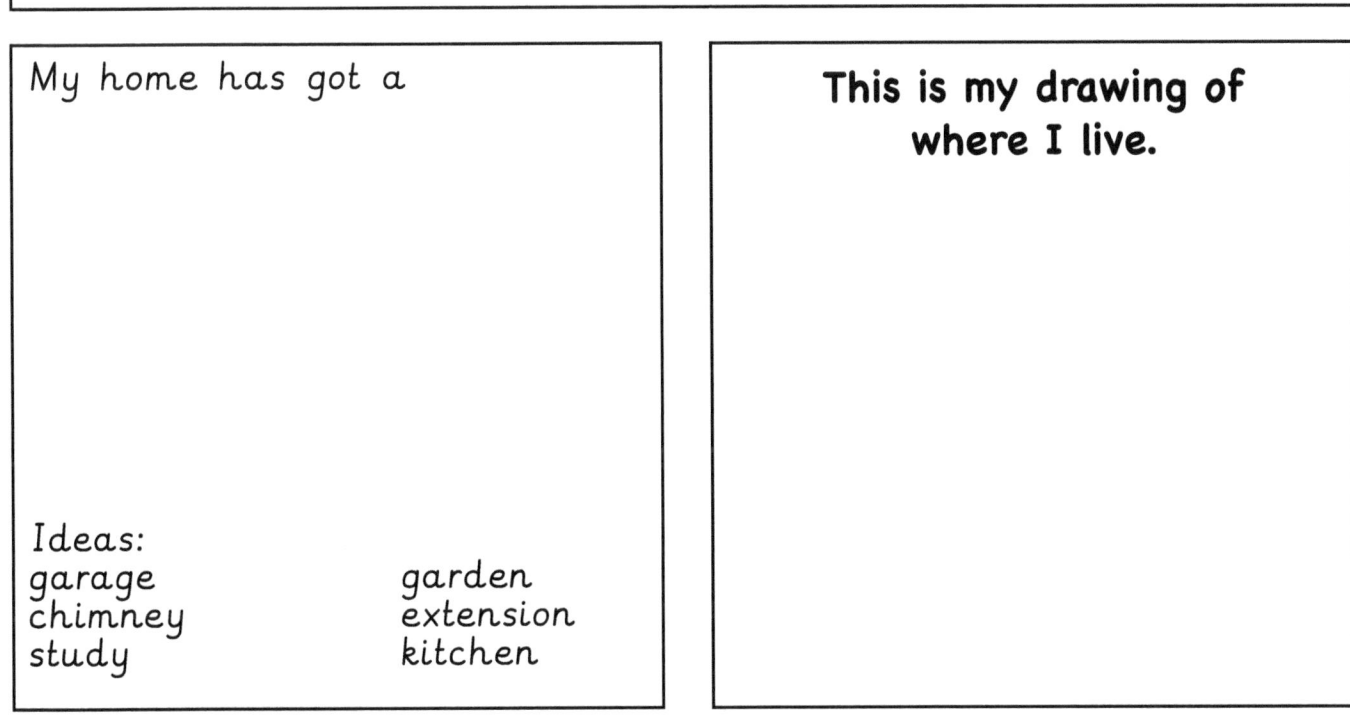

Descriptive account

My dad

This is my drawing of my dad.

My dad has _____ brother(s) and _____ sister(s).

Ideas: no   one   two   three   four

My dad likes to

and

play football | read a paper | bake a cake | cut the grass

My mummy

This is my drawing of my mummy.

My mummy has _____ hair.

Ideas:
brown   black   blonde
ginger   long   short

My mummy likes to

and

read a book

walk the dog

sing a song

ride a bike

My friend

My friend has

hair   brown   black   blonde   ginger

long   short   curly   straight   bunches

eyes   blue   brown   grey

My friend

wears glasses   has freckles

My friend has

brother(s)?   sister(s)?   how old?

pets?   dog?   cat?   goldfish?   rabbit?

My friend is good at   **My friend likes**

drawing   PE   doing sums   playing football

I like my friend because

makes up... games to play
chooses... to be my partner
listens... to my secrets
invites me... for a play date
shares...   sweets

Who am I?

Descriptive account

What do I look like?

hair brown   black   blonde   ginger

long   short   straight   curly   bunches

eyes blue   brown   grey

glasses

freckles

rosy cheeks

Who is in my family?

brother(s)?   sister(s)?   how old?

What pets do I have?

rabbit?   goldfish?   cat?   dog?

Where do I live?

What are my favourite things?

favourite food?   toy?   book?   film?

What am I good at?
What is the most exciting thing that I have done?
Is there anything I am not so keen on?

This year I am most looking forward to

Boost Creative Writing, Years 1–2
© Judith Thornby and Brilliant Publications Limited

My day as a Victorian child

Descriptive account

I will put on

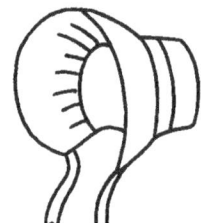   

a bonnet   a flat cap   a long dress   my boots

At school I will

 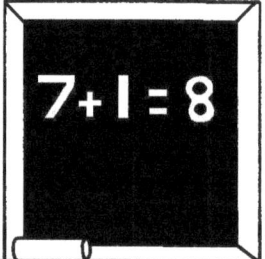 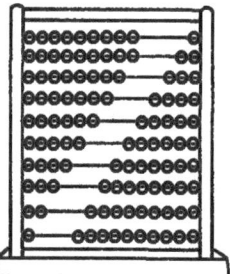 

write on a slate   look at a blackboard   use an abacus   be scared of the cane

Then I will play with

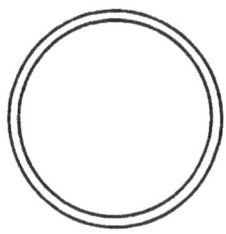  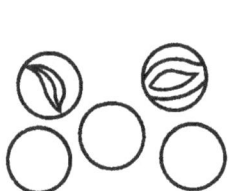 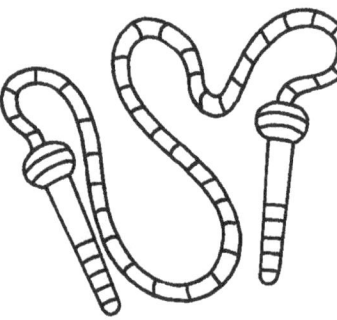

a hoop   a hobby horse   marbles   skipping rope

After that I will

  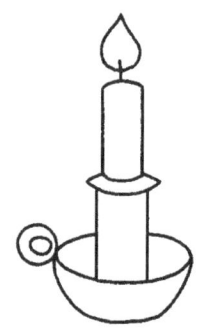

use a washboard to wash my clothes   put a warming pan in my bed   light a candle

This page may be photocopied for use by the purchasing institution only.

Boost Creative Writing, Years 1–2
© Judith Thornby and Brilliant Publications Limited

My dream party

Where will you go? How? What will you do?

Deep under the sea

dolphin palace   swim with mermaid
collect shells   stare at the fish   eat shark cake

On the moon

rocket   hot air balloon   paint a star
dance with an alien   eat moon cookies

In nursery rhyme land

paint a rainbow   unicorn   sit on Humpty's   run after a
                             wall   gingerbread man

It will be…

I will go with…

We will get there on a…

Then we will…

At teatime I will eat…

Finally I will…

Autumn – I can see

Collect leaves, conkers and other things you find in the autumn.

I can see

Autumn – I can see

Possible WOW words

brown yellow crispy dry	leaves	floating fluttering like kites dancing like ballerinas swirling like a snowstorm rustling crunching under my foot
juicy shiny spiky rosy smooth fat	berries conkers apples acorns pumpkins	growing waiting
busy sleepy/drowsy/dormant	squirrels flocks of... hedgehogs	looking for flying sleeping
sparkling wet	frost dew	lying

Create a fairy tale

Start: Once upon a time...
Setting
Characters: good, bad/naughty
Some trouble caused by bad character
Good character saves the day
End: they all live happily ever after

Setting

Ideas:
dark gloomy cave
cottage in the wood

beautiful castle/palace
deep under the sea

Characters

Ideas:
happy pixie
generous fairy
bad dragon
sea monster

beautiful princess
kind mermaid
wicked witch

sad giant
handsome prince
naughty elf

Story
What happens to the good person?

Ideas: is put under a spell
gets captured
Who helps? How?

loses something special
gets lost
has a trick played on him/her

What happens in the end?
(How is it all sorted?)
They all live happily ever after

Create a fairy tale

Use the story mountain format to help you plan your fairy tale.

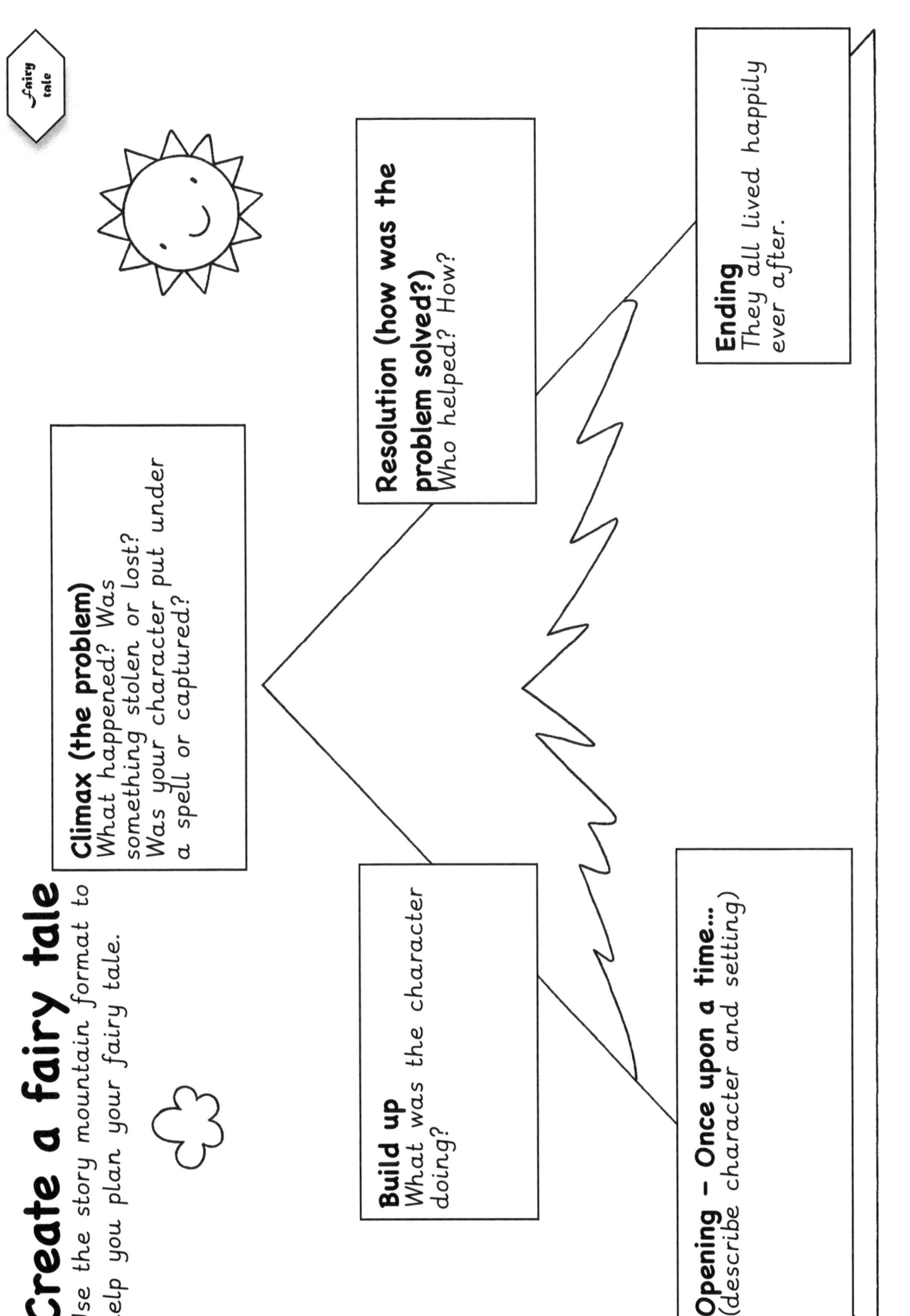

Climax (the problem)
What happened? Was something stolen or lost? Was your character put under a spell or captured?

Resolution (how was the problem solved?)
Who helped? How?

Build up
What was the character doing?

Ending
They all lived happily ever after.

Opening – Once upon a time...
(describe character and setting)

Boost Creative Writing, Years 1–2
© Judith Thornby and Brilliant Publications Limited

This page may be photocopied for use by the purchasing institution only.

Create a character for a fairy tale

Draw and colour a picture and then write about the character.

Who?

Ideas:
elf   mermaid   wizard   fairy   witch
princess   giant   sea monster   dragon   prince

What does your character look like?
Ideas:
size:	tall	short	plump	tiny	little
hair	eyes	ears	body	tail	wings
crown	shoes	wand	dress	pretty	beautiful
straight	curly	long	short	blonde	black
blue	silver	golden	scaly	pointed	sparkling

How does your character behave?
Ideas:
friendly   naughty   gentle   generous   kind hearted   untidy
funny   forgetful   greedy   lonely   wicked   shy

What does your character like doing?
Ideas:
making spells, playing tricks, collecting shells, combing her hair

Fairy tale character template

Create a character for a fairy tale.

My character is _____ .

Create a setting for a fairy tale

Draw and colour a picture and then write about the setting.

Where?
What does it look like?

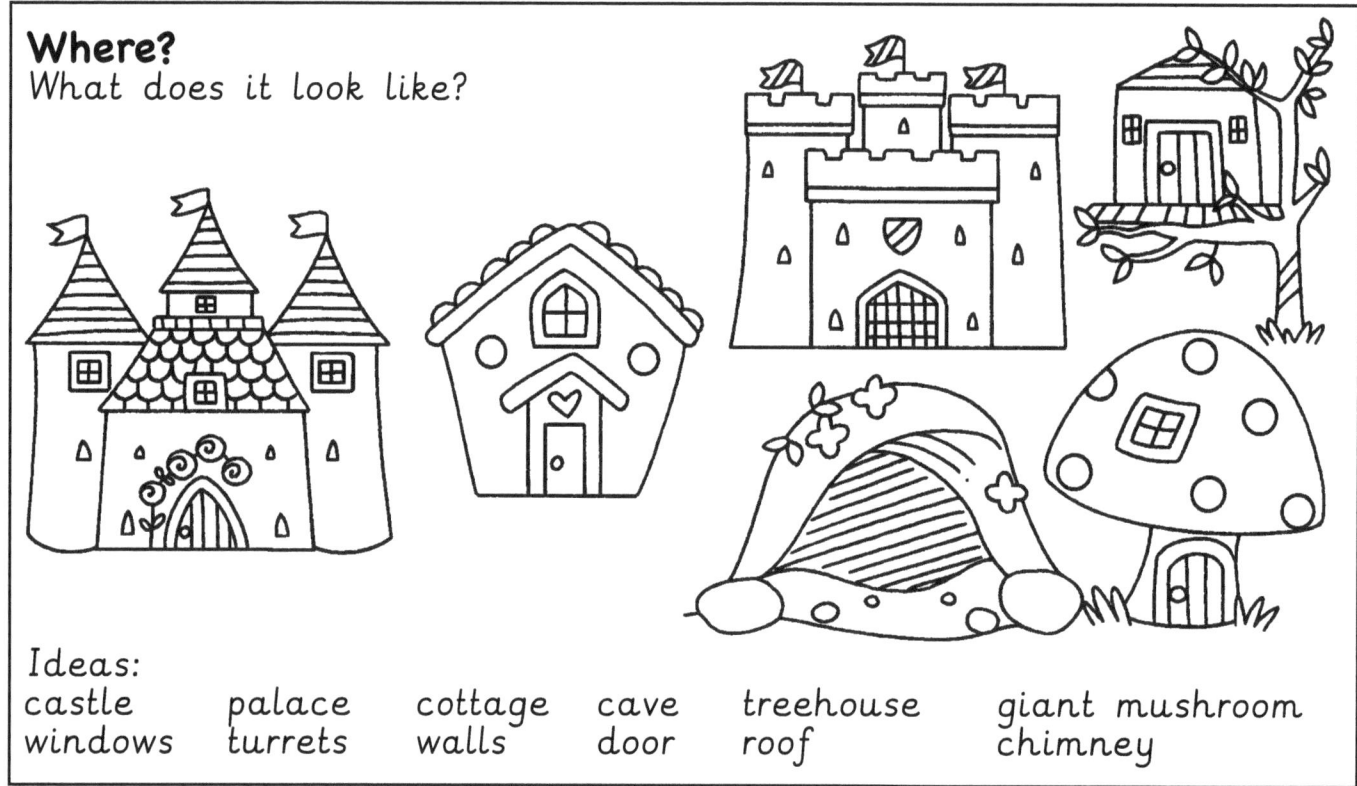

Ideas:
castle   palace   cottage   cave   treehouse   giant mushroom
windows   turrets   walls   door   roof   chimney

Where is it?

Ideas:
on top of a hill   in a wood   in a forest
on an island   deep under the sea

What is near it?

Ideas:
lake   moat   fountain   garden   tall trees   little path
garden   flowers   fruit bushes   hedge   high wall   mountain
hill   shells   shipwreck   lobster pot coral reef

This page may be photocopied for use by the purchasing institution only.

Boost Creative Writing, Years 1–2
© Judith Thornby and Brilliant Publications Limited

Fairy tale setting template

Create a setting for a fairy tale.

My setting is _____ .

The super mini-beast

Draw and colour a picture of a marvellous mini-beast.

Add labels

| wings | legs | body | antennae | spotty | hairy |
| striped | short | long | yellow | blue | orange |

What does it like to do?

Ideas:
flies   slithers   eats   collects   looks for   rests   wriggles

My pet monster

Draw, colour and label a picture of your monster.

Name of monster:
_____

Use WOW words

Ideas:				
body	eyes	snout	fangs	tentacles
antennae	legs	webbed feet	claws	horn
scales	wings	tail	hairy	spotted
striped	spiky	pointed	smooth	

My pet monster

My monster is called _____.

What does your monster look like?

Ideas:
size?	shape?	colour?		
eyes	eyelashes	ears	body	snout
fangs	tentacles	wings	horn	tail
scales	fur	webbed feet		

Where does he sleep?
What's his bed like? What type of covers does his bed have?

Ideas:
in the attic
inside the shed
under a bush in the garden

What is his character like?
What does he do if he is happy? What does he do if he is angry?

Ideas:
shy   friendly   nervous   easy-going   turns invisible
glows   makes a noise like...

What do you feed him? How much?
Be imaginative!

Ideas:
... four fat juicy worms from the garden, covered in ketchup

How long have you had him? Why is he special?

Ideas:
helps me with my homework
plays games with me

This page may be photocopied for use by the purchasing institution only.

Boost Creative Writing, Years 1–2
© Judith Thornby and Brilliant Publications Limited

It's time to go out

Write a story about a tiny person who went to see his or her friend in a very odd way. Be imaginative!

What time was it?

It was...

in the middle of the night   early in the morning

Who?

How does he/she travel? Where is the transport found?

Write about three amazing things seen on the way.

Ideas:
Who?   What was it doing?   Then what happened?

Idea number 1:
... passed a cloud and saw a spotted green bird. He was chasing a black cat. The cat had stolen an egg from his nest.

What happened when the person got to his/her friend's house?

 # It's time to go out

Draw, colour and label a mind map of your ideas. Be imaginative.

When does the tiny person travel? How? Where does he/she find the transport?

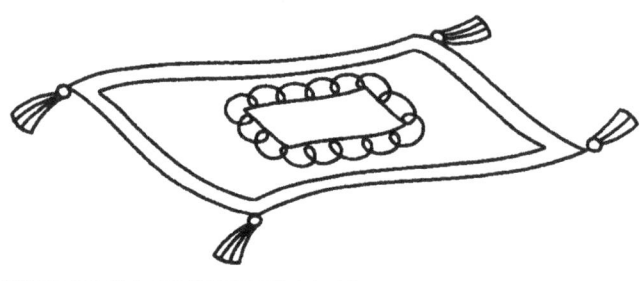

What three amazing things does he/she see on the way?

Our trip to the seaside

We went on a trip to the seaside.

First
How did we get there?

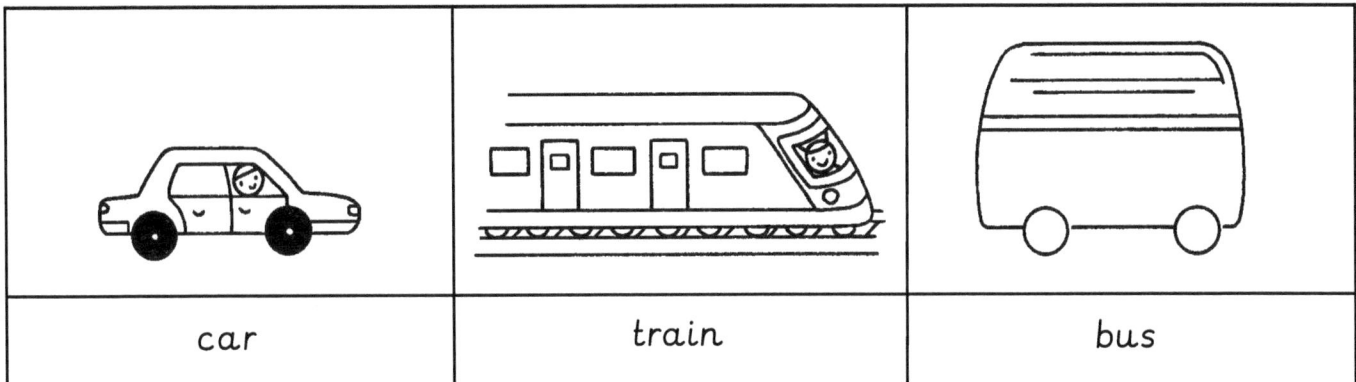

Then
What did we do?

After that
What did we eat?

Finally
What happened at the end? How did we get home?

Victorian seaside

Bessie and Albert went to the seaside.

First
What did they do first?

| made a sandcastle | changed in a bathing hut | paddled in the sea |

Then
What did they do?

| had a donkey ride | saw a Punch and Judy show | ate an ice cream |

After that
What did they do?

| went to the pier | penny slot machines | heard the band playing |

Finally
What happened at the end? How did they get home?
Idea: Did they go by steam train?

The story of Grace Darling

Write about the story of brave Grace Darling who helped her father one stormy night in 1838.

Who was Grace Darling?
Where did she live?

What happened one night?
What did she see that worried her?

What happened next?
How did she help?

Describe the rescue
Ideas:

clinging to rocks   blankets   cold and tired

What happened afterwards?

The story of Grace Darling

Use some of these words to help you write your report.

Who was Grace Darling?
lived
Farne
father
island
Longstone
lighthouse
busy
helped
strong
rower

What happened one night?
7th September 1838	wrecked	early one morning
sinking	terrible storm	large hole in the ship
ship	people clinging to	slippery rocks
trouble	drowning	

What happened next? Describe the rescue
saw danger	scared
begged father	fingers blue with cold
rowing boat	rescued
swamped by waves	nine people still alive
storm raged	made two trips

What happened afterwards?
survivors
safe
exhausted
looked after
so grateful
medal
bravery
risked her own life

Useful connecting words
After a while
Suddenly
Then
Meanwhile
Eventually
At last

This page may be photocopied for use by the purchasing institution only.

The story of Emily Davison

Write about Emily Davison, a 'lawless lassie', who wanted women to be able to vote.

Who was Emily Davison?
(Was she a suffragette?)

Emily Davison was born in 1872.

She was...

What did she want women to have?
(Did she break the law to get attention?)

Emily Davison wanted women over 21 to have a...

She got into trouble because...

One day
(What did Emily do at Epsom Racecourse? Did she do it to get publicity?)

Emily ducked under the barrier on the race course track and...

Then...? After that?
(What happened to Emily at Epsom Racecourse? Did the horse trample her?)

Finally
(Was the law changed?)

The law was changed in...

The story of Emily Davison

Use some of this information to help you write your story.

born in London in October 1872
very bright student
took classes at university but wasn't allowed to get a degree as she was a woman
worked as a governess and a teacher

thought all people should be equal
wanted votes for women
joined suffragettes
unlawful acts to attract publicity
given nickname 'the lawless lassie'
went to prison many times

38 years old in 1913
Derby Day
ducked under barrier at Epsom Racecourse
grabbed bridle of King George V's horse
tried to pin 'Votes for women' sash on the horse
horse trampled her
died four days later in hospital

In 1928 all women over 21 allowed to vote

The story of Rosa Parks

Write about Rosa Parks who, on one day in 1955, refused to be treated unfairly any longer.

Who was Rosa Parks?
Where did she live?

Rosa Parks was born in 1913.

She lived in…

What was the law on the buses in the 'deep south' of United States up to 1956?

The law up to 1956 on the buses was…

One day
(Why was Rosa Parks on the bus? What did she do?)

Rosa refused to…

Then… After that…
She was taken to _____ for the night.

(Did African Americans refuse to use the buses in support?)

Finally
(Did the bus company lose money?)

The law was changed in…

The story of Rosa Parks

Use some of these words to help you write your story.

born in 1913
lived in Alabama in 'deep south' of United States
African American (black)
worked as a seamstress

special law – Jim Crow law – made it legal to discriminate against black people
segregation
seats on bus reserved for white people
if not enough seats for white people, black people had to give up their seats

long day at work
very tired
riding home on bus
no seats for a white person
spent night in jail
expected to give up her seat

did not think it fair
refused
broke the law
arrested
had to pay fine

in support of Rosa Parks
across country
many African Americans
formed civil rights group
wanted everyone to be treated fairly
led by Martin Luther King
refused to use buses until law was changed
bus company lost money
law finally changed in 1956
Rosa became a national hero

Christopher Columbus

Write about Christopher Columbus who discovered a 'new world'.

Who was Christopher Columbus?
He was born in 1451.
He lived in…
He went to sea when he was…

Where did he want to travel? Why?
He wanted to travel to…

(Did Queen Isabella of Spain give him the money to travel?)

One day
He was in command of three ships called…

They set sail and discovered…
(Where did he think he had gone?)
He thought he had sailed to…

Then
(How many voyages did he make to the 'new world'?)

He made _____ voyages.

Finally
(Why is he remembered?)

Christopher Columbus is remembered because…

Information report

Christopher Columbus

Use some of these words to help you write your report.

born in 1451
lived in Italy and Portugal
sailor – went to sea as a teenager
great explorer

wanted to sail to India, China and Japan
rich in gold, spices and jewels
Queen Isabella of Spain gave him money
not easy – few maps

sailed west
command of three ships: the Pinta, the Niña and the Santa María
landed in America
discovered the Caribbean islands of Jamaica and Trinidad
New World
called people 'Indians'
thought he had landed in India
claimed land for Spain
made four voyages altogether

died in 1506
remembered as a skilled sailor and navigator
first European person to visit new lands
people in Europe started to travel to North and South America

The first man on the moon

Write about Neil Armstrong who ws the first man ever to step on the moon.

Who was Neil Armstrong?
(When was he born? Where did he live? What was his job?)

Neil was born in...

He became an...

His spaceship was called...

One day in 1969
(What did he do? Where was he going? How long did it take?)

He was going to...

It took him ____ days to reach the moon.

Then he got into the lunar module
(What was the surface of the moon like?)

It was difficult to land on the moon because...

On the moon
He collected...

Finally he left the moon
(When did he get back to earth? Are his footsteps still visible on the moon? Why?)

The first man on the moon

Use some of these words to help you write your report.

Neil Armstrong
born in 1930
lived in Ohio in America
always wanted to be a pilot
flew over 200 types of aircraft
passed difficult tests
became an astronaut
captain of Apollo 11 spaceship
wanted the challenge of going to moon

blasted off from Kennedy space centre in Florida
July 1969
three day journey to the moon
boarded lunar module (Eagle) to get down to the moon

landed safely
difficult landing
had to avoid huge boulders, some the size of small cars
climbed out of module
'that's one small step for man, one giant leap for mankind'
on moon for 21 hours
nearly ran out of fuel
collected moon rocks

mission went well
3 days later module landed in Pacific Ocean

national hero
America had won the race to put the first man ever on moon
footprints still on moon – thick dust no wind

A letter to Santa

Dear Santa,

I have been good because I

I would like

I have left you a _____ and

_____ for the reindeer.

Love from,

Boost Creative Writing, Years 1–2
© Judith Thornby and Brilliant Publications Limited

This page may be photocopied for use by the purchasing institution only.

57

Letter/ Review

A letter to Santa

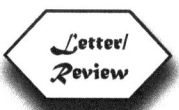

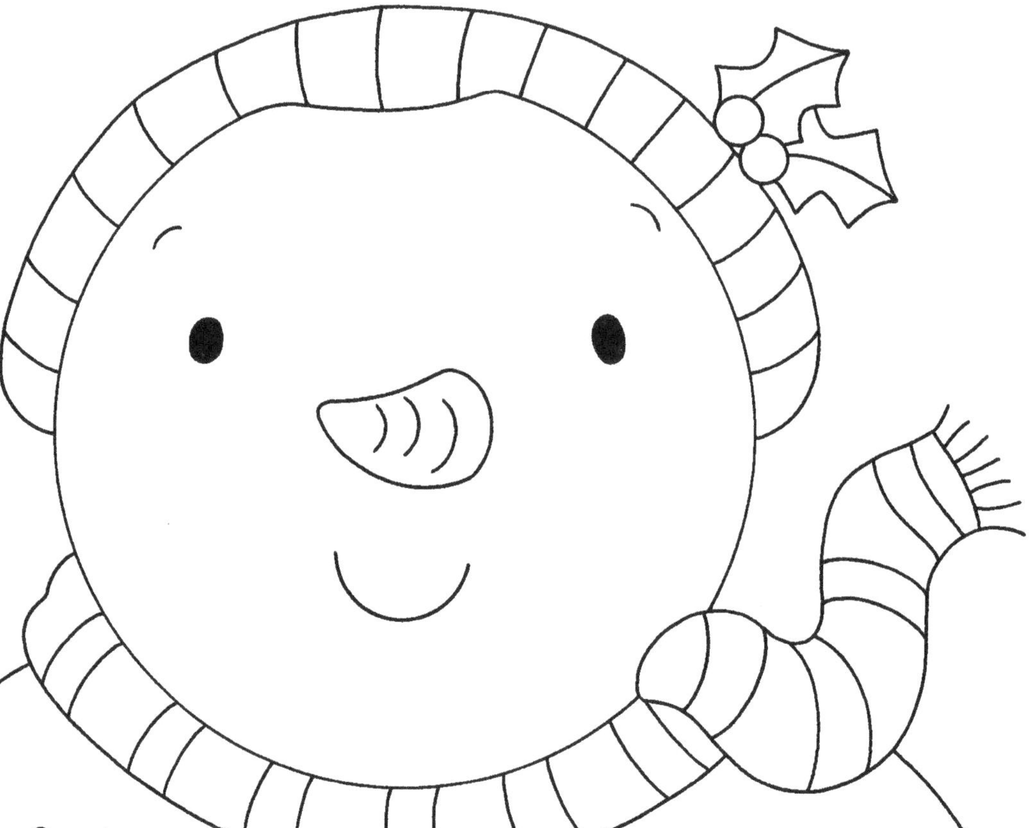

Dear Santa,

I have been good because I

I would like

I have left you a ______________________ and

______________________ for the reindeer.

Love from,

Book review

Title

Author

What was the story about?

Who was your favourite character and why?

Which part of the story did you like best?

Who would like this story?

How many stars would you give this book?

A review of Year 2

Interesting starting sentence

Ideas:
It has been good fun in Year 2.
I have really enjoyed Year 2.

What have you done so far? Why did you like doing it?

Ideas:
trip to...
class assembly
performance

What are your favourite lessons? Why?

Is there anything you are not so keen on? Why?

What are you getting better at?

What will you miss when you go up into Year 3?

What are you looking forward to in Year 3?

Ideas:
new lessons   teachers

Rain

Write a rhyming poem about the rain. Use the words in bold as the first line in each rhyming pair. Write the next line. Don't forget it must end with a rhyming word.

For example:
Split spl<u>at</u>
I will not sit on the m<u>at</u>.

Use this sheet to think of lots of rhyming words.

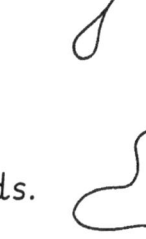

Split spl<u>at</u>

My rhyming words

Drip dr<u>op</u>

My rhyming words

Splish spl<u>ash</u>

My rhyming words

Splash spl<u>ish</u>

My rhyming words

Pitter p<u>atter</u>

My rhyming words

You can use these words!

h<u>at</u>	c<u>at</u>	sh<u>op</u>	h<u>op</u>	d<u>ash</u>
m<u>ash</u>	f<u>ish</u>	w<u>ish</u>	ch<u>atter</u>	m<u>atter</u>

Rain

by ....

....

....

....

....

....

....

....

....

....

My home

What do you like to do in your home?

I like to .... in the	/k/ cook camp cry
I like to .... in the	/l/ lie down laugh
I like to .... in the	/h/ hop help

Choose a room:
living room   hall   bedroom   dining room
toilet   kitchen   cloakroom   study

I like to .... in the	☐
I like to .... in the	☐
I like to .... in the	☐
I like to .... in the	☐
	☐

Grandad

Write a funny rhyming poem. Create a pretend conversation between a child and a grandad who is deaf.

For example:
Tom: Do you want me to get your cap?
Grandad: No, the cat is on my lap.

Tom: Shall I go and get us a cake?
Grandad: No, do not get a snake!

Tom: Can I buy you a drink?
Grandad: No, I do not need a new sink.

Tom: Are you feeling well?
Grandad: Yes, I think I can spell.

Start by working out words with the same rhyming patterns. Then think of your sentences. Here are a few to start you off:

ap	nap map clap trap cap lap
ake	cake bake flake Jake lake rake
ink	drink pink rink sink think wink
ell	bell sell shell smell well yell

This page may be photocopied for use by the purchasing institution only.

Boost Creative Writing, Years 1–2
© Judith Thornby and Brilliant Publications Limited

Grandad

by ....

..........................: ....

Grandad: ....

..........................: ....

Grandad: ....

..........................: ....

Grandad: ....

..........................: ....

Grandad: ....

..........................: ....

Grandad: ....

Boost Creative Writing, Years 1–2
© Judith Thornby and Brilliant Publications Limited

Fireworks

Play around with 'noisy' words and make up a fireworks poem.

For example:
Bang Zoom Boom
Beautiful fireworks
Glittering in the night sky.

Fizzle Sizzle Whizz
Silvery sparklers
Swirling brightly in my hand.

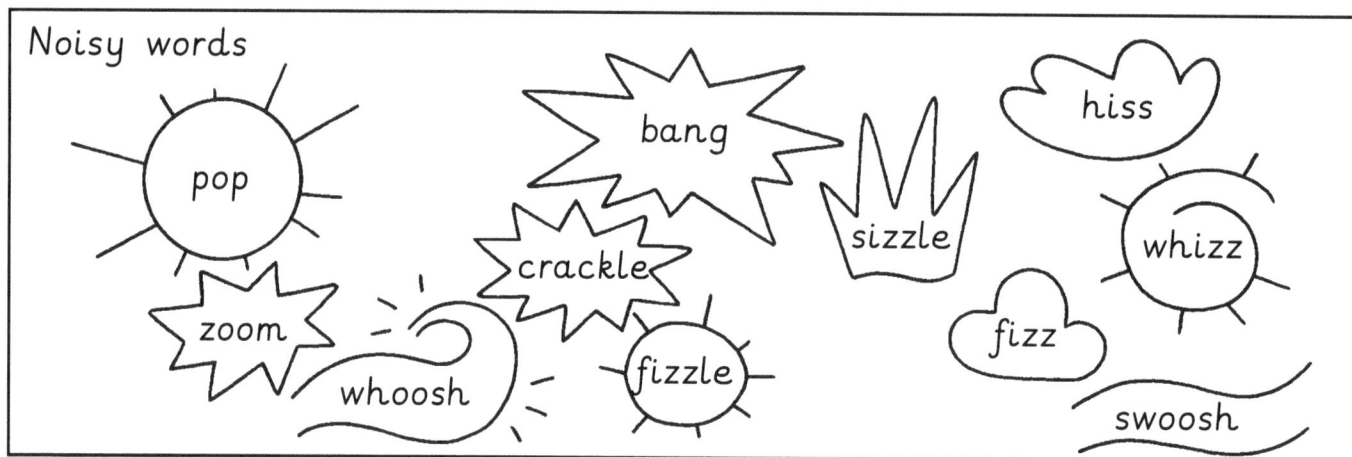

Try to work out your ideas before you write.
Here are some useful words:

colourful amazing	rocket	shooting up blasting off
silvery shining bright	sparks sparklers	glittering sparkling glowing
frightening loud	fire crackers	exploding
beautiful amazing	Roman candle	swirling
wonderful marvellous	Catherine wheel	whizzing around twisting
red hot huge	bonfire	crackling
dark	night sky	appearing disappearing
happy excited	children	admiring loving the sight

This page may be photocopied for use by the purchasing institution only.

Fireworks

by ....

_____

....

....

_____

....

....

_____

....

....

_____

....

....

Noisy words: pop, bang, sizzle, hiss, crackle, whizz, zoom, fizz, whoosh, fizzle

Mini-beasts

Where is it?

on a leaf next to a...	under a stone under a...	in the grass beside the...	by the plant pot near the...

What is it?

ant bee beetle butterfly caterpillar centipede daddy long legs	dragon fly earthworm earwig frog grasshopper green fly ladybird	mosquito moth slug snail spider wasp worm

What is it doing?

buzzing following fluttering flying	getting gliding guarding looking for	resting returning to scurrying scuttling	searching for sleeping slithering wriggling

Choose a WOW word

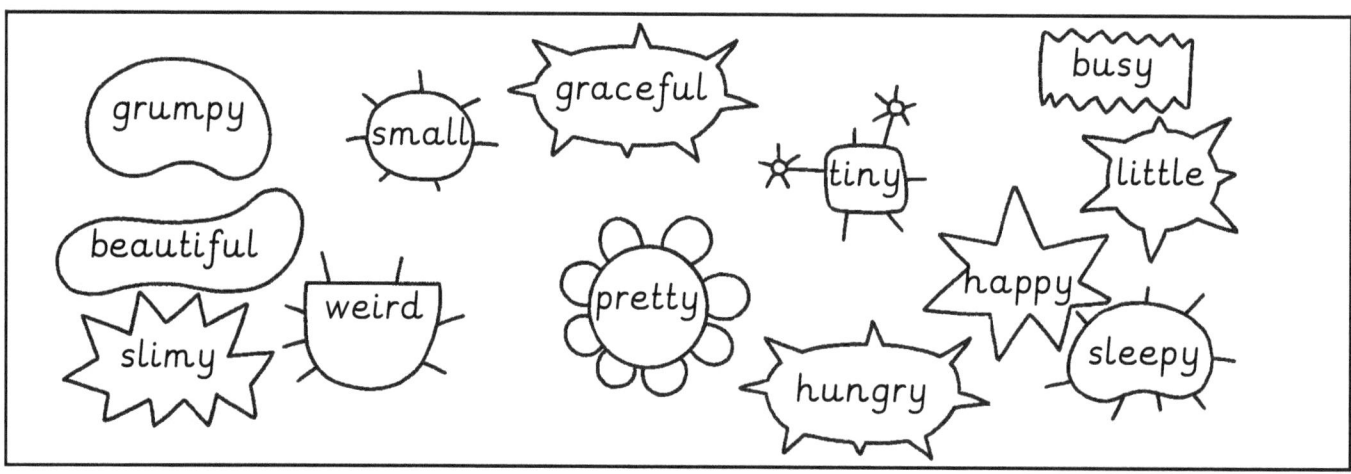

grumpy, small, graceful, busy, tiny, little, beautiful, weird, pretty, happy, slimy, hungry, sleepy

Make up sentences:
Under a flower pot a small woodlouse is sleeping.

Mini-beasts

by _____

Spring

What can you see?

| tulip | daffodil | grass | blossom | growing flowering peeping budding |

What can you see?

 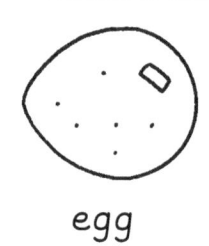 

| bird | egg | worm | nest building hatching wriggling |

What can you hear?

| chicks | bee | frog | croaking cheeping buzzing |

Choose a WOW word

round, red, long, fresh, yellow, busy, hungry, beautiful, pretty, little, tiny, new, happy, slimy

Make up poem ideas:

New grass growing

Red tulip _____

_____

I can see spring is here.

Spring

by _____

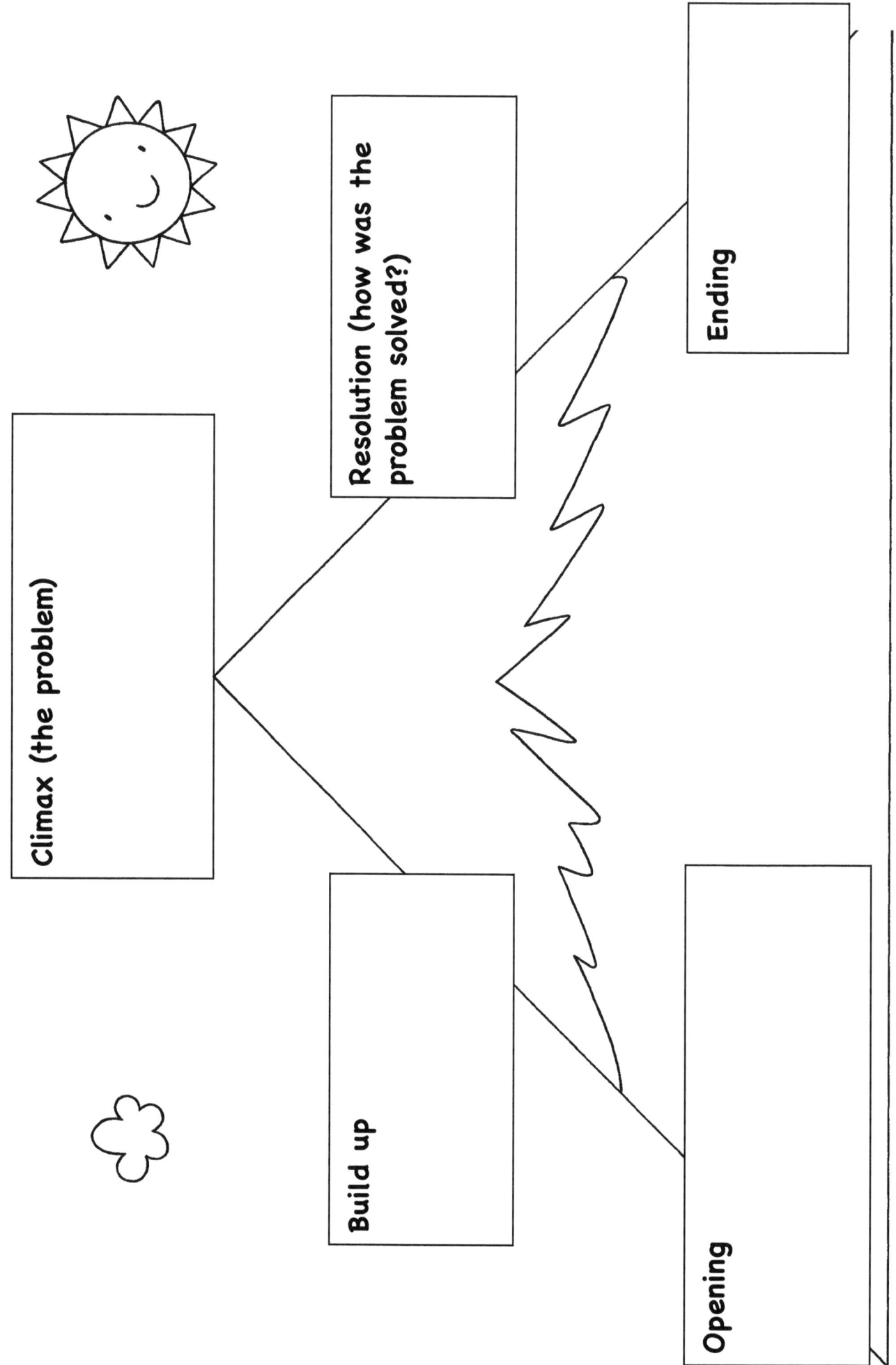

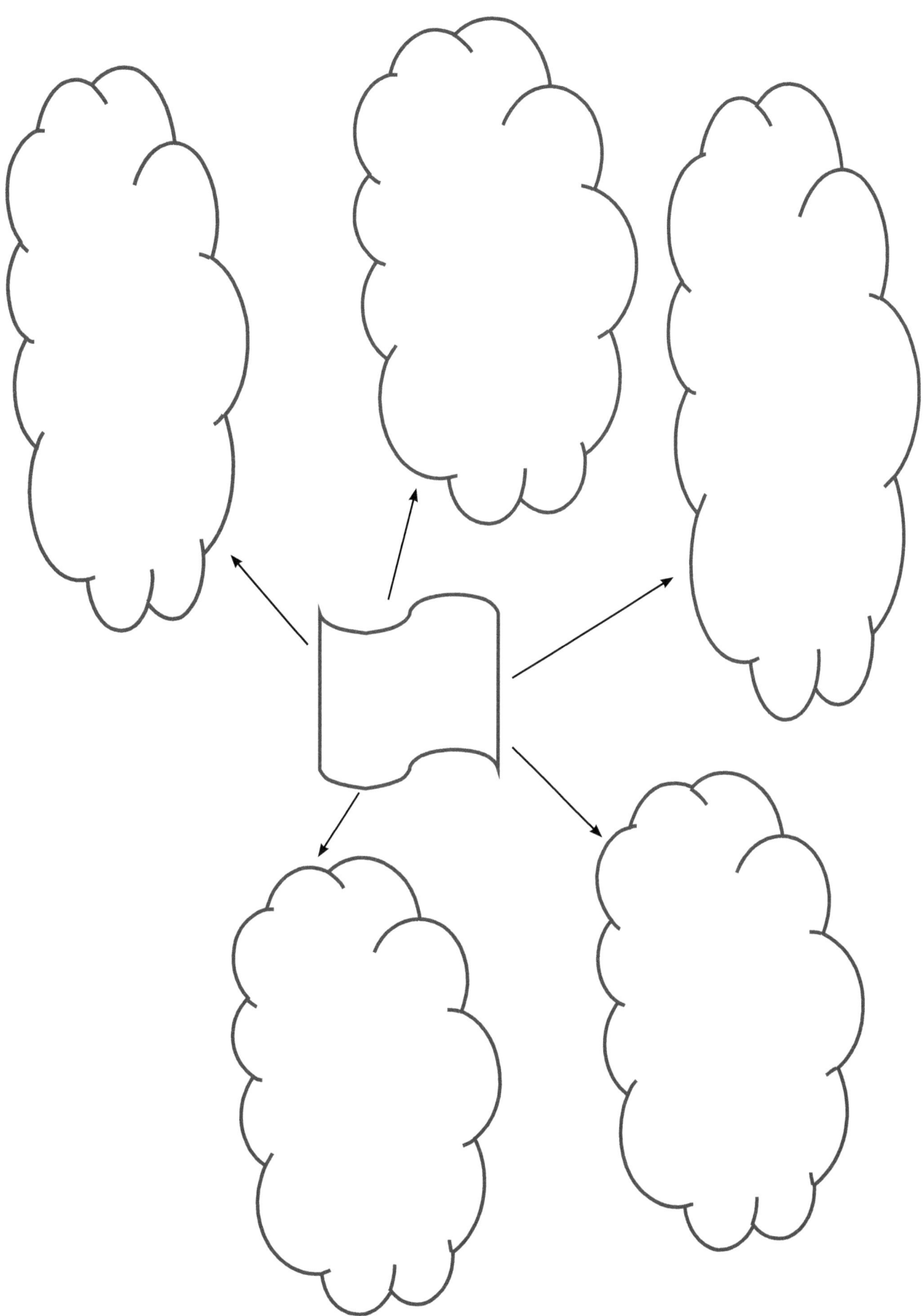

www.ingramcontent.com/pod-product-compliance
Ingram Content Group UK Ltd.
Pitfield, Milton Keynes, MK11 3LW, UK
UKHW050728220625
459968UK00009B/182